THE ONE NEW MAN

That the Gentiles Should be fellow heirs

LESLIE M. JOHN

ISBN: 978-0-9882933-2-8

THE ONE NEW MAN

That the Gentiles
Should be fellow heirs

LESLIE M. JOHN

Contents

THE ONE NEW MAN

CHAPTER 1

GOSPEL OF GRACE

The Gospel of Grace was preached by the disciples of Jesus Christ, Apostle Paul, Silas, Barnabas, Timothy etc.

Their ardent service to Lord Jesus Christ, and the persecutions they suffered while proclaiming the Gospel of Jesus Christ in various regions, in Israel and outside Israel, were recorded in the Book of Acts.

Apostle Paul was minister of Gospel of Jesus Christ to the Gentiles, and through his ministry many Gentiles accepted Lord Jesus Christ as their personal Savior.

After Death, Burial and Resurrection of Lord Jesus Christ, and before His ascension to heaven, the Lord commanded them to wait at Jerusalem until Holy Spirit descends from Heaven and indwell them, and give power to them to preach the Gospel.

Apostle Paul made extensive journeys in Israel, Syria, Turkey, and Greece, and the details of his visit to several regions proclaiming Gospel of Jesus Christ are recorded in the Book of Acts. These regions included many Gentile territories.

Some interpret that until the time period that came to fruition as in Acts 28:28 there was no Church and all those who were converted were grafted into Jewish faith, and later became Christians.

The argument I based on Acts 28:28 which reads…

"Be it known therefore unto you, that the salvation of God is sent unto the Gentiles, and *that* they will hear it" (Acts 28:28 KJV), and on Acts 28:31 which reads…

"Preaching the kingdom of God, and teaching those things which concern the Lord Jesus Christ, with all confidence, no man forbidding him" (Acts 28:31 KJV)

Therefore, some argue that all those who were converted before Acts 28:28 period do not belong to Church, but belong to the "Kingdom".

Their belief is that all those who came to the LORSD were proselytized just as in Old Testament and only thereafter, Gospel of Jesus Christ was preached.

A case in point in the Old Testament was of Ruth, who was a Moabite woman acknowledged the God of Israel and her God, and thus was proselytized to become Jew first.

Similar were many strangers who left Egypt along with the children of Israel were subsequently proselytized when they accepted the God of Israel and their God.

While that interpretation as relates to Old Testament was true, it is not true in the case of New Testament believers.

The Gospel of Jesus Christ is specifically about the substitutionary death and resurrection of Jesus Christ and the belief exercised by sinner that Jesus Christ as his/her Lord and believe in heart that God raised Him from the dead on the third day. It is then that a sinner saved by grace through faith in Him.

The Book of Acts contains historical facts of Apostles, primarily that Apostle Peter and Apostle Paul. The Book of Acts contains the historical transition of the "Kingdom" message to the message of 'One New Man" the "CHURCH", whose head is Lord Jesus Christ with members from Jews and Gentiles.

However, Apostle Paul's writing to Ephesians as we read in Ephesians 3:3-6 shows that the Gentiles were made fellow heirs before the end of Acts period.

"How that by revelation he made known unto me the mystery; (as I wrote afore in few words, Whereby, when ye read, ye may understand my knowledge in the mystery of Christ) Which in other ages was not made known unto the sons of men, as it is now revealed unto his holy apostles and prophets by the Spirit; That the Gentiles should be fellow heirs, and of the same body, and partakers of his promise in Christ by the gospel" (Ephesians 3:3-6 KJV)

 The transition could be seen from:

1. Preaching of Gospel in Jerusalem ("And the word of God increased; and the number of the disciples multiplied in Jerusalem greatly; and a great company of the priests were obedient to the faith" Acts 6:7)

2. Preaching of Gospel in Judea and Samaria ("Then had the churches rest throughout all Judaea and Galilee and Samaria, and were edified; and walking in the fear of the Lord, and in the comfort of the Holy Ghost, were multiplied". Acts 9:31)

3. Preaching of Gospel in Tyre and Sidon (Herod was smitten by God and the Church is blessed. "But the word of God grew and multiplied". Acts 12:20-24)

4. Preaching of Gospel in Asia Minor ("And so were the churches established in the faith, and increased in number daily" Acts 16:5)

5. Preaching of Gospel in Europe ("And this was known to all the Jews and Greeks also dwelling at Ephesus; and fear fell on them all, and the name of the Lord Jesus was magnified" Acts 19:17) and 6. Preaching the Gospel in Europe:

(a) "Be it known therefore unto you, that the salvation of God is sent unto the Gentiles, and [that] they will hear it" Acts 28:28

(b) "Preaching the kingdom of God, and teaching those things which concern the Lord Jesus Christ, with all confidence, no man forbidding him" Acts 28:31)

Some have differentiated Acts 28:28 and Acts 28:31 and misinterpreted during the period of Acts conversion was by 'grafting' about which Paul spoke in Romans Chapters 9-11 took place.

That is to say all those who were converted to Christianity during the period of Acts were spiritually grafted into Good olive trees as wild olive branches would be physically 'grafted' into the good olive trees. It would also mean that they first became Jews inasmuch as Abraham was believed to be the olive tree and the branches drew sap from the root, which is symbolic of drawing faith from Abraham.

That would also mean there was no Church during Acts period. They do not believe that the Church came into existence in the period about which there is record in Acts Chapter 2, wherein it is mentioned about Holy Spirit coming down from heaven and empowering the disciples to preach the Gospel of Jesus Christ.

The Gentles saved during Acts period were not circumcised to become proselytes. In Christ circumcised and un-circumcised are all equal members of the Church.

Peter, James, Mark, Paul and Barnabas were as much equal members of the Church as any other Gentile, who believed in Jesus Christ as his/her personal Savior.

If it is argued that there is no Church during Acts period, then it goes to say that Peter and Paul were also not members of the "Body of Christ".

"Having abolished in his flesh the enmity, even the law of commandments contained in ordinances; for to make in himself of twain one new man, so making peace" (Ephesians 2:15)

Let us read two verses before we go into the details of the "one new man". The phrase "new man" has different meaning than that of "one new man".

"And that ye put on the new man, which after God is created in righteousness and true holiness". (Ephesians 4:24)

"And have put on the new man, which is renewed in knowledge after the image of him that created him" (Colossians 3:10)

NEW MAN

Those verses in Ephesians 4:24 and Colossians 3:10 point towards the one who has accepted Lord Jesus Christ as personal savior and become 'new man' having put off the old man in him. He is a new creation in Christ Jesus. God considers him as righteous and holy. He is renewed in the knowledge of God who created him.

THE ONE NEW MAN

The phrase "one new man" referred to in Ephesians 2:15 is the one body of Christ that has members from Jews and Gentiles. They are made one in Christ and there is no difference between them.

There are few conditions that need to have been fulfilled before 'one new man' came into existence.

Firstly, the condition "Having abolished in his flesh the enmity, even the law of commandments contained in ordinances" should have been fulfilled.

Secondly, the one becoming part of that "one new man" should have been cleansed of his sin through the blood of Lord Jesus Christ. That is to say the person who becomes a member of that 'one new man' should have repented of his/her sin and accepted Lord Jesus Christ as his/her personal Savior.

Then, obviously the 'one new man' also can be called member of the "Church", "the body of Christ" and the "Bride of Christ". Thirdly, the condition "to make in himself of twain" should have been fulfilled.

THE FIRST CONDITION

Was it after Acts 28:28 or is it when Jesus was crucified on the cross? Obviously, the condition was fulfilled when Jesus was crucified on the cross.

"Jesus, when he had cried again with a loud voice, yielded up the ghost". (Matthew 27:50)

The veil in the Temple was rent into two from top to bottom, opening the way from Holy to the Holies and earth did quake and rocks rent. (Matthew 27:51)

The centurion and others who were with him, watching Jesus saw the earthquake and things that have happened at that time and greatly feared and acknowledged that Jesus was the "Son of God" (Matthew 27:54)

Jesus rose from the dead on the third day (Matthew 28:6), and after forty days he ascended into heaven and will come back again in the same manner he ascended into heaven. (Acts 1:9-11)

SECOND CONDITION

Bible says we all, irrespective of whether we are Jews or Gentiles, have sinned and come short of the glory of God (Romans 3:9, 23) and the wages of sin is death but the gift of God is eternal life through Jesus Christ our Lord. (Romans 6:23)

To become partakers of God's blessing and to receive salvation one has to repent of his/her sins and accept Jesus Christ as personal savior. Bible says:

"That if thou shalt confess with thy mouth the Lord Jesus, and shalt believe in thine heart that God hath raised him from the dead, thou shalt be saved" (Romans 10:9)

"If we confess our sins, he is faithful and just to forgive us our sins, and to cleanse us from all unrighteousness". (1 John 1:9)

THE THIRD CONDITION

Whoever has accepted Lord Jesus Christ as his personal savior, whether we be Jews or Gentiles, whether we be bond or free, have been made to drink of one spirit and for by one Spirit we are all baptized into one body. (1 Corinthians 12:13)

THE ONE NEW MAN

JESUS BECAME OUR HIGH PRIEST

"For we have not an high priest which cannot be touched with the feeling of our infirmities; but was in all points tempted like as we are, yet without sin". (Hebrews 4:15)

The barrier between Jews and Gentiles was removed. That is to say, the provision for 'one new man' was made immediately when Jesus was crucified on the cross.

Now the question is when exactly the Jews and Gentiles became one. Was it after Acts 28:28 or is it when Jesus was crucified on the cross?

When the day of Pentecost was fully come as we read in Acts Chapter2 there were in Jerusalem Jews, devout men, out of every nation under heaven.

"And there were dwelling at Jerusalem Jews, devout men, out of every nation under heaven". (Acts 2:5)

Also in Acts 2:9-11 there is a mention of all those who were present from different regions.

"Parthians, and Medes, and Elamites, and the dwellers in Mesopotamia, and in Judaea, and Cappadocia, in Pontus, and Asia, Phrygia, and Pamphylia, in Egypt, and in the parts of Libya about Cyrene, and strangers of Rome, Jews and proselytes, Cretes and Arabians, we do hear them speak in our tongues the wonderful works of God". (Acts 2:9-11)

The people present there when Peter spoke of Jesus starting from Acts 2:14 were from Judea and from those who dwell at Jerusalem. Note how the scriptures clearly distinguish those who were present in Jerusalem as from "Judea" and "all ye that dwell at Jerusalem".

If only Jews were there at that time, the distinction should not have been made, but the scriptures clearly distinguish two categories of people present at the time when Peter spoke about Jesus of Nazareth.

Those who were present in Jerusalem during the time of Pentecost were empowered to speak about Lord Jesus Christ. Holy Spirit, who is the "Promise of the Father", came upon all those who were commanded by Lord Jesus Christ to wait at Jerusalem until Holy Spirit came upon them. Acts 2:4 says:

"And they were all filled with the Holy Ghost, and began to speak with other tongues, as the Spirit gave them utterance".

When this news was heard abroad, multitudes came together and were confused because every man heard them speak in his own language and they all understood one another.

They were all amazed and marveled and said to each other, "...Behold, are not all these which speak Galileans? And how hear we every man in our own tongue, wherein we were born?" (Acts 2:1-8)

Paul quotes Hosea Chapter 1 and says in Romans 9:25 that those Israelites who were unfaithful to God were called "Not my people" by God.

They were all Gentiles. But what about those who were not the descendants of Jacob, who were present in Jerusalem at the time when Peter spoke of Jesus? Were there no Roman Government officials?

How sure is anyone to say that those who were called "Parthians, and Medes, and Elamites, and the dwellers in Mesopotamia, and in Judaea, and Cappadocia, in Pontus, and Asia, Phrygia, and Pamphylia, in Egypt, and in the parts of Libya about Cyrene, and strangers of Rome, Jews and proselytes, Cretes and Arabians" were also the descendants of Jacob.

I Chronicles Chapter 1: 17-28 have the details of sons of Shem, Elamites, and many others. Neither scriptures nor the history records of Flavius Josephus show that all those were descendants of Jacob. They were all Gentiles.

There is no basis to say that those three thousand saved when Peter preached were only Jews or descendants of Jacob.

There are some who say without producing any evidence that they were mixed generations from Jacob's descendants and pure Gentiles and there are some who say that they were all from "House of Israel" who mixed up with Samaritans without showing where those from "House of Israel" were or are now.

Some try to make up some stories even from those narrations which are mystery.

"Then they that gladly received his word were baptized: and the same day there were added unto them about three thousand souls". (Acts 2:41)

Later many more souls from Jews and Gentiles were added to the Church.

"Praising God, and having favour with all the people. And the Lord added to the church daily such as should be saved" (Acts 2:47)

CHAPTER 2

PETER'S MESSAGE

When Peter spoke of Jesus of Nazareth that He was a man approved of God, he had full knowledge of Jesus, because Peter was a disciple of Jesus Christ.

Peter knew that Mary was the earthly mother of Jesus and Joseph had purposed earlier to put her off when Joseph came to know that Mary was pregnant. Jesus was born of the Virgin Mary of the Holy Spirit (Matthew 1:20).

Later in his life Peter wrote in his 1 epistle Chapter 1 a great message honoring "God the Father of our Lord Jesus Christ, who has begotten us unto a lively hope by the resurrection of Jesus Christ from the dead to an inheritance, and undefiled, and that fades not, which is reserved for us". (1 Peter 1:3-5)

This Peter, an Apostle of Jesus Christ said in Acts 2:21-24 that whosoever shall call on the name of the Lord shall be saved.

This Peter addressed the men in Israel and testified about Jesus of Nazareth that he was approved of God and did miracles and wonders and signs. Peter said that they took Jesus, who was delivered by the determinate counsel of foreknowledge of God, and killed him and that God raised Him from the pains of death, which could not hold him Jesus ascended into heaven and seated on the right hand of the Father and will come back after all his enemies are brought to His footstool.(Acts 2:21-25, 31, Psalm 16:8-11). Peter also quoted the David and his prophecy about Jesus Christ. (Psalm 110:1)

Before Peter went to meet Cornelius, an uncircumcised Gentile, a devout man, who feared God and gave much alms, and also prayed to God always, God taught a lesson to Peter.

It was when Peter was still thinking about Mosaic Law and ordinances. Even though he was hungry he had determination not to eat that which was forbidden under Mosaic Law and Ordinances.

Jesus had already ascended into heaven by this time, and the Apostles had already begun preaching the Gospel of grace. It was not the kingdom message that they were preaching, but the Gospel of Grace.

The message was that Jesus was crucified by sinful people like me, and that he died for saving the sinner, and that he was buried and rose on the third day from the dead and after forty days ascended into heaven. Peter was the first one to preach about this fact as we read in Acts Chapter 2.

Later in Acts Chapter 9 there is narration of how Paul, who persecuted Christians, was encountered by Jesus, who said that He was the one whom Paul was persecuting. When Christians are persecuted Jesus felt that he was being persecuted.

It was this Lord Jesus Christ, the Son of God, the very God himself, who said to Peter to go to Cornelius to give him the salvation message. Before going to Cornelius, Peter saw a man named "Aeneas" sick of palsy at Lydda. Peter said to him "...Jesus Christ maketh thee whole: arise, and make thy bed. And he arose immediately" (Acts 9:34).

Because of this miracle done by Peter in the name of Jesus, many turned to the Lord. Later Peter prayed and raised Tabitha (also known as Dorcas) from the dead. Many believed in the Lord.

PETER STAYS IN THE HOUSE OF TANNER

Then Peter went to Simon, who was a tanner, and stayed with him for many days. Jews considered themselves as 'clean' and treated Gentiles as "unclean". In this case Peter did not have any hesitation to stay for many days in the house of an unclean tanner, Simon who was a Jew, rather than in the house of Cornelius, who was a clean Gentile.

"And it came to pass, that he tarried many days in Joppa with one Simon a tanner". (Acts 9:43)

CORNELIUS'S VISION

Cornelius saw an angel of God in a vision saying to him that his prayers and his alms to people were honored by God. The angel of God said to Cornelius that he should send word for Simon Peter (the disciple of Lord Jesus Christ), who stayed in the house of one named Simon, who was a tanner. Cornelius sent two of his servants to Joppa to call for Simon Peter. (Acts 10:1-8)

TANNER

A 'tanner' is the one who deals with dead animals. International Standard Bible Encyclopedia describes 'Tanner' as:

Quote: "tan'-er (burseus, from bursa "a hide"): The only references to a tanner are in Ac 9:43; 10:6,32. The Jews looked upon tanning as an undesirable occupation and well they might, for at best it was accompanied with unpleasant odors and unattractive sights, if not even ceremonially unclean.

We can imagine that Simon the tanner found among the disciples of Jesus a fellowship which had been denied him before.

Peter made the way still easier for Simon by choosing his house as his abode while staying in Joppa. Simon's house was by the seashore, as is true of the tanneries along the Syrian coast today, so that the foul-smelling liquors from the vats can be drawn off with the least nuisance, and so that the salt water may be easily accessible for washing the skins during the tanning process.

These tanneries are very unpretentious affairs, usually consisting of one or two small rooms and a courtyard. Within are the vats made either of stone masonry, plastered within and without, or cut out of the solid rock. The sheep or goat skins are smeared on the flesh side with a paste of slaked lime and then folded up and allowed to stand until the hair loosens.

The hair and fleshy matter are removed, the skins are plumped in lime, bated in a concoction first of dog dung and afterward in one of fermenting bran, in much the same way as in a modern tannery. The bated skins are tanned in sumach (Arabic summak), which is the common tanning material in Syria and Palestine. After drying, the leather is blackened on one side by rubbing on a solution made by boiling vinegar with old nails or pieces of copper, and the skin is finally given a dressing of olive oil.

In the more modern tanneries degras is being imported for the currying processes. For dyeing the rams' skins red (Ex 25:1-40) they rub on a solution of qermes (similar to cochineal; see DYEING), dry, oil, and polish with a smooth stone" Unquote.

Bible emphasizes Peter's stay in the house of a tanner: When Bible mentions specifically an incidence it is not without any significance. It needs serious consideration.

"And it came to pass, that he tarried many days in Joppa with one Simon a tanner". (Acts 9:43)

"He lodgeth with one Simon a tanner, whose house is by the sea side: he shall tell thee what thou oughtest to do". (Acts 10:6)

It was one just before Peter spoke to Cornelius, who was a Roman uncircumcised Gentile from Italian Band. Cornelius was baptized later. Points to note Tanning is unclean. Tanner is unclean. Gentiles were unclean in the sight of Jews. Yet God said what he called as 'clean' man should not call it as 'unclean'.

Hebrew Strong's Number 2931 is "tame' " transliterated as "taw-may' "

In KJV the word "Unclean" is mentioned as defiled, 5; infamous, 1; polluted, 1; pollution, 1; unclean, 79

Greek Strong's number 169 transliterated as "Akathartos" is found in KJV as

KJV (30) - foul, 2; unclean, 28;

"Or if a soul touch any unclean thing, whether it be a carcase of an unclean beast, or a carcase of unclean cattle, or the carcase of unclean creeping things, and if it be hidden from him; he also shall be unclean, and guilty". Leviticus 5:2 and also there are more details about dietary restrictions imposed on the children of Israel. These instructions included that they shall eat the beasts that have parted hoof, cloven-footed and Chew the cud. But they shall not eat

Camel because he chews the cud, but has no divided hoof
Coney because he chews the cud, but has no divided hoof
Hare because he chews the cud, but has no divided hoof
Swine because he chews the cud, but has no divided hoof

God said the children of Israel shall not eat their flesh and they shall not touch their carcasses. They are all considered as 'Unclean" by God. (Leviticus 11:2-8)

PETER'S VISION

On the morrow when the servants of Cornelius were reaching the city, Peter went upon the housetop to pray. It was about sixth hour and Peter was very hungry. Before he went to eat with Tanner, he saw a vision. In the vision he saw heaven opened and a certain vessel descending towards him.

It was like a great sheet knit at the four corners and let down to the earth. The sheet contained variety of animals; four-footed beasts, wild beasts, creeping things and fowls of the air.

Peter heard a voice saying to him to rise, kill and eat. But Peter refused to eat because there were animals that were prohibited to be eaten as per Mosaic Law and ordinances.

Peter said that he had never eaten that which is common or unclean. The voice said to him second time, and Peter refused to eat.

The voice said to Peter that what God had cleansed should not be called common by him. This was done three times and the sheet was retrieved into heaven. (Acts 10:10-16)

PETER MEETS CORNELIUS

While Peter was in trance and thought on the vision, the Spirit spoke to him and said to him that three men were seeking him. Peter was asked to arise and go with them without doubting. Peter obeyed the voice and went with the men to Cornelius and said that he was Peter.

Just before Peter identified himself Cornelius fell on the feet of Peter and worshipped him; but Peter lifted him and said that he was also a man.

He meant that God is the only One who is to be worshipped and none else. Peter saw in the home of Cornelius many others who were there to listen to him. Peter, who was a Jew, asked Cornelius, who was an un-circumcised Gentile, as to why he sent word for him knowing fully well that it was unlawful for Jew to keep company with Gentile.

Cornelius said to Peter that he saw a man in bright clothing stood before him four days ago when he was fasting and said to him that his prayers were honored and his alms were recognized by God.

Cornelius continued saying that the man, whom he saw, asked him to send word for Peter, specifically mentioning the name as Simon, whose name was Peter, and who was staying with a 'tanner'.

That is the reason why he called for him and said that they were all there to hear what God had to say to all of them in his house.

SALVATION TO CORNELIUS

After Peter spoke to the congregation consisting people from various nations and tongues the message of salvation as we read in Acts Chapter 2, when the Holy Spirit fell on them and they all talked in many languages that could be understood by everyone, the gospel of Jesus Christ that peter gave to Cornelius, a Gentile, was a full message of grace, whereby a person can have salvation.

Peter spoke saying with God there is no partiality and that whoever works righteous and fears God is accepted by Him. Peter said that Jesus of Nazareth is the Lord of all, and that preached peace unto the children of Israel and the baptism that John preached. The word was published throughout Judea from Galilee.

Jesus of Nazareth did miracles and healed the sick after he was anointed with the Holy Spirit and with power. Jesus also cast away evil spirits from those who were oppressed of the devil.

Peter testified that The Father in heaven was with Jesus, the Son of God, and that the disciples were all witnesses to the preaching, and miracles of Jesus of Nazareth.

They were witnesses to all that they saw in the land of Jews, and in Jerusalem, and yet Jesus was killed and he was hung on the Cross.

God raised Jesus the third day and He appeared to all of them on different occasions and ate and drank with them.

Peter said that Jesus asked them to preach to people that He was ordained of God to be the Judge of the quick and the dead.

All the prophets spoke about Jesus and whoever believes in Him shall receive remission of sins. While Peter was still speaking Holy Spirit fell on all of them that heard the Gospel of Jesus Christ.

The Jews, and the brethren, who came with Peter, were surprised to see that Holy Spirit fell on all of them to whom Gospel of Jesus Christ was preached. They all spoke in tongues and magnified God.

Then Peter asked if there is any obstruction for them to be baptized in the name of the Lord and commanded them to be baptized in the name of the Lord. They requested Peter to stay with them for few more days. (Acts 10:19-48)

 Apostles and brethren, who were in Judea, heard that Gentiles also received the word of God and they spoke in tongues.

When Peter went to Jerusalem they argued with him as to why he went to Gentiles and ate with them. Their questioning was based on the instructions of Jesus who earlier said to them that they should not go in the way of Gentiles.

"These twelve Jesus sent forth, and commanded them, saying, Go not into the way of the Gentiles, and into any city of the Samaritans enter ye not" (Matthew 10:5)

Peter recollects this after Cornelius receives salvation that God was teaching him a lesson that whether it be Jew or Gentile, circumcised or un-circumcised, everyone who receives salvation is equal in the sight of God and none is 'common' or 'unclean'.

Peter rehearsed before them the entire vision when he saw 'common' and 'unclean' animals in a vessel on a sheet that descended from heaven and a voice asked him to rise, kill and eat them; and that he refused. But the voice said to him that he should not call as 'common" and "unclean" that which God has cleansed (Acts 11:1-10).

DID CORNELIUS BECOME JEW OR CHRISTIAN?

Cornelius became Christian, a member of the "CHURCH" (Ekklesia).

Salvation to Gentiles was already in the plan of God. Israel is blinded in order that Gentiles may receive salvation. (Romans 11:6-8, 2 Corinthians 3:14)

Isaiah's prophecy was fulfilled by Jesus.

"That it might be fulfilled which was spoken by Esaias the prophet, saying, Behold my servant, whom I have chosen; my beloved, in whom my soul is well pleased: I will put my spirit upon him, and he shall shew judgment to the Gentiles.

He shall not strive, nor cry; neither shall any man hear his voice in the streets. A bruised reed shall he not break, and smoking flax shall he not quench, till he send

THE ONE NEW MAN

forth judgment unto victory. And in his name shall the Gentiles trust". (Matthew 12:17-21, Cf. Isaiah 42:3)

Abraham, who was the father of faith, was the root of Olive Tree. Gentiles, who are compared to wild Olive Tree, believed in Jesus as their savior, the unbelieving Jews were cut off and believing Gentiles were grafted into the Natural Olive Tree in their places and thereby Jews and Gentiles are made one in Christ.

They became the body of Christ, and they are all collectively called the "bride" of Christ'. The Gentiles who believed Jesus as their savior were saved by grace through their faith in Jesus and became partakers of the root who is Abraham, who was known as father of faith.

Both Abraham's descendants through Isaac, and Jacob, the believing Jews, along with unbelieving Gentiles are now the members the 'Church", whose head is Lord Jesus Christ, who identified himself as the true "vine".

"And if some of the branches be broken off, and thou, being a wild olive tree, wert grafted in among them, and with them partakest of the root and fatness of the olive tree" (Romans 11:17)

Apostle Paul's analogy of wild olive branches being grafted into natural olive tree is to mean that the Gentiles are made equal partners in the spiritual blessings along with Jews. Some of the natural branches were cut off because of their unbelief and in their place the wild olive branches are grafted.

This is also not to mean that to accommodate Gentiles in the natural olive tree the branches of the natural branches were cut off, but because of their unbelief that the Jews, who are considered as natural olive branches, were cut off.

The wild olive branches are asked not to take pride in themselves because they were grafted into natural olive tree. Paul warns that if natural branches were cut off because of their unbelief, God will not hesitate to cut off wild olive branches.

This does not mean that salvation will be lost by any believer in Christ, but it only means that they will be cut off to make way for the natural branches.

Paul argues if God had cast away the natural branches and says "God forbid".

"I say then, Hath God cast away his people? God forbid. For I also am an Israelite, of the seed of Abraham, of the tribe of Benjamin" (Romans 11:1)".

Here neither Peter nor Paul said that the Gentiles who believed in Jesus became first Jews and then Christians, but they were saved by grace through faith in Jesus Christ, and therefore, they became Christians.

The argument is that by faith exercised by Jew or Gentile in Jesus Christ had the same impact on them; nothing less and nothing more than becoming one in the Lord Jesus Christ. Jews and Gentiles became one in Christ and Gentiles have become partakers of the faith of Abraham.

THE ONE NEW MAN

There is no difference whether it is Jews or Gentiles, they are all one in Christ right from the period in Acts Chapter2 when three thousand were added to the Church, and Acts Chapter 10, where we see about salvation that was granted to an uncircumcised Gentile, Cornelius as also to others who were with him, and now and even until Jesus comes again to take his bride away.

"Then they that gladly received his word were baptized: and the same day there were added unto them about three thousand souls". (Acts 2:41)

"While Peter yet spoke these words, the Holy Ghost fell on all them which heard the word. And they of the circumcision which believed were astonished, as many as came with Peter, because that on the Gentiles also was poured out the gift of the Holy Ghost. For they heard them speak with tongues, and magnify God. Then answered Peter" (Acts 10:44-46)

The Church came into existence in Acts Chapter2 and the "One New Man" is the Church, which has members from Jewish community and from Gentiles. They are all one in Christ.

"So we, *being* many, are one body in Christ, and every one members one of another" (Romans 12:5 KJV)

There is neither Jew nor Greek, there is neither bond nor free, there is neither male nor female: for ye are all one in Christ Jesus. (Galatians 3:28)

CHAPTER 3

SALVATION TO

GENTILES

The brethren at Puteoli who heard of Paul and others went to meet them at cities called 'Appii forum' and 'The three taverns'.

Paul thanked God because he was very near to Rome and he took courage. On their arrival at Rome the Centurion delivered the prisoners to the captain guard but the Centurion with the help of a soldier took care of Paul. (Acts 28:15-16)

It was Paul's opportunity, then, to speak to the Christians at Rome and defend his position. Paul spoke to the men and brethren at Rome that he was innocent of the charges that were leveled against him.

He did neither mislead nor did work against the customs of the fathers, yet he was imprisoned and brought from Jerusalem to Rome to stand before Caesar.

Earlier he was examined of the charges leveled against him and they found that he did nothing that deserved death penalty. Jews laid grievous complaints against Paul, but they could not prove. But when Jews spoke against him he was constrained to appeal to Caesar. Festus, willing to show favor to Jews asked Paul if he would like to go to Jerusalem for trial but Paul asked that he may be sent to stand at Caesar's judgment seat.(Acts 25:7-12)

Paul was a Roman citizen, a Pharisee, Hebrew of Hebrews, a Jew by birth of the tribe of Benjamin (Philippians 3:5). Earlier Paul was arrested at Jerusalem because he was proclaiming that Jesus was the Son of God. Jews thought Paul was speaking blasphemy. Paul also taught that circumcision was not required for salvation. Jews took serious exceptions to his teachings. Paul was held prisoner for two years at Caesarea.

"But after two years Porcius Festus came into Felix' room: and Felix, willing to shew the Jews a pleasure, left Paul bound." (Acts 24:27)

Paul did not mean to offend Jews nor accuse them because of their false allegations leading to his apprehension but he was defending himself that he did nothing that deserved punishment. At Rome Paul called Jews to let them know of these facts.

Paul's speech was filled with hope for the disturbed Israel and said that he was bound in chains for this reason. But when they heard of Paul's speech they said that they did not receive any letter from Judea or heard any word about Paul from any of the brethren.

Yet, they desired to hear from Paul about the entire situation and about the Jews of whom there was a bad talk all over.

The Jews there set apart a day for Paul to speak and expound of the matters that were of much concern to them and their sect.

This was obviously very interesting situation and many gathered to listen to Paul. Making use of the opportunity he was given, Paul spoke elaborately about Jesus from out of the Law of Moses, and out of the prophets from morning till evening.

As it usually happens everywhere, even now, some believed Paul's exposition and some did not believe. The Jews did not agree with one another among themselves and some of them did not believe what Paul spoke of Jesus.

"Saying, Go unto this people, and say, Hearing ye shall hear, and shall not understand; and seeing ye shall see, and not perceive: For the heart of this people is waxed gross, and their ears are dull of hearing, and their eyes have they closed; lest they should see with their eyes, and hear with their ears, and understand with their heart, and should be converted, and I should heal them." (Acts 28:26-27 KJV)

The prophesy was in Isaiah 6:9-10 which reads as "And he said, Go, and tell this people, Hear ye indeed, but understand not; and see ye indeed, but perceive not.

Make the heart of this people fat, and make their ears heavy, and shut their eyes; lest they see with their eyes, and hear with their ears, and understand with their heart, and convert, and be healed"

Lord Jesus Christ quoted this prophesy earlier to Jews as we read in Matthew 13:14

"And in them is fulfilled the prophecy of Esaias, which saith, By hearing ye shall hear, and shall not understand; and seeing ye shall see, and shall not perceive"

"But though he had done so many miracles before them, yet they believed not on him: That the saying of Esaias the prophet might be fulfilled, which he spake, Lord, who hath believed our report? and to whom hath the arm of the Lord been revealed?

Therefore they could not believe, because that Esaias said again, He hath blinded their eyes, and hardened their heart; that they should not see with their eyes, nor understand with their heart, and be converted, and I should heal them" (John 12:37-40)

 Paul was upset at this point of time and said that the "salvation of God is sent unto the Gentiles, and they will hear it".

The Jews departed and reasoned among themselves. Paul was at Rome for two whole years in his hired house, and spoke of the kingdom of God to all those who visited him at his home. He taught them about

Lord Jesus Christ with boldness and no man forbad him from speaking about Jesus.

Acts Chapter 28 or any other scripture does not give more details of Paul's ministry afterwards or as to what happened to his life. Secular history says that he died as a martyr for Christ.

There are few points that need our attention here. When Paul said that salvation of God was sent to the Gentiles was it the first time that Gentiles heard of Lord Jesus Christ either from others or from Paul? No, Peter spoke of Lord Jesus Christ to Cornelius as we read in Acts Chapter 10.

Was Cornelius Jew or Circumcised? No, Cornelius was not a Jew and he was not circumcised to be considered as a Proselyte.

Was he grafted into Jews based on Paul's exposition that we read in Romans Chapter 11 Yes, but his grafting into the Natural branches was not anything special or of more importance than any other Gentile! All Gentiles who are considered as grafted based on the exposition of Romans Chapter 11 are just as equal in status as we are as "One New Man" as Cornelius was.

Nothing in the scriptures suggests that the grafting of Gentiles in Acts period was of any extra importance or of less importance than that of those Gentiles who are saved after the Acts period.

"And when he had found him, he brought him unto Antioch. And it came to pass, that a whole year they assembled themselves with the church, and taught much people. And the disciples were called Christians first in Antioch. " (Acts 11:26)

When Jews rejected Paul's preaching as we read in Acts Chapter 13 the Gentiles requested him that the word of God may be preached to them.

On the next Sabbath Paul spoke to the Gentiles and they heard the word of God. Jews took objection to Paul's preaching but Paul and Barnabas were bold enough to speak about Jesus and that led to Jews getting envy of Paul and contradicted him.

When there was a difference of opinion among Jews and religious proselytes Paul and Barnabas spoke to them and persuaded them to continue in the grace of God (Acts 13:43).

Paul said to them that it was necessary that the word of God be spoken to them first and then to Gentiles and he did that exactly as Jesus commanded him to do.

Some say that all these Gentiles saved during the Acts period were the descendants of Jacob, but there is no convincing evidence to show that they were all descendants of Jacob.

"For so hath the Lord commanded us, saying, I have set you to be a light of the Gentiles that you should be for salvation unto the ends of the earth." (Acts 13:47)

Earlier, Jesus had compassion on Centurion as we read in Matthew Chapter 8 and on Canaanite woman as we read in Matthew Chapter 15.

No doubt Jesus came to seek the lost sheep of Israel but his coming was not with absolute negligence toward Gentiles.

Jesus resisted his disciples going in the way of Gentiles as we read in Matthew Chapter 10, yet his concern for Gentiles was not with absolute negligence toward them, otherwise, the most familiar verse John 3:16 would have been of no consequence.

"For God so loved the world that he gave his only begotten Son, that whosoever believeth in him should not perish, but have everlasting life". (John 3:16)

THE ONE NEW MAN

CHAPTER 4

ISRAEL

God named Jacob as Israel and loved Israel more than we can imagine. He has called Israel as His first born son.

It is not a name given by human but it is the name that is given by God; it is "Israel", which in Hebrew means God has striven, or God has saved.

"And he said, Thy name shall be called no more Jacob, but Israel: for as a prince hast thou power with God and with men, and hast prevailed." Genesis 32:28.

The descendants of Jacob are Israel. To be specific, the tribe of Judah, and the tribe of Benjamin, and those, who are from the tribe of Levi, who have joined with Judah are called, 'Jews'; and the rest of them are called, "Israel".

God has given great privilege to the "Israel" as a whole to be called as His first born.

"And thou shalt say unto Pharaoh, Thus saith the LORD, Israel is my son, even my firstborn" Exodus 4:22

A woman stricken with devil approached Jesus for healing of her daughter, crying "O Lord, thou Son of

David; my daughter is grievously vexed with a devil" but Jesus replied, " ... I am not sent but unto the lost sheep of the house of Israel." Matthew 15:24.

However, because of her faith in acknowledging her lowliness, when she said to Jesus, " yet the dogs eat of the crumbs which fall from their masters' table", "Then Jesus answered and said unto her, O woman, great is thy faith: be it unto thee even as thou wilt. And her daughter was made whole from that very hour".

The woman was gentile; her plea was heard by Jesus because He had compassion on her. This is a mystery not seen in the Old Testament.

God blessed Abraham and said, whoever blesses Abraham will be blessed and whoever curses Abraham will be cursed, and likewise, God gave the privilege to Israel only to be called as Israel.

Whoever calls himself/herself a 'Jew' or 'Israel', and not a Jew or Israel will face the anger of the Lord. "I know thy works, and tribulation, and poverty, (but thou art rich) and I know the blasphemy of them which say they are Jews, and are not, but are the synagogue of Satan". Revelation 2:9.

It is very serious to identify oneself as "Jew" when one is not a Jew. Jacob and his descendants had all the priority in the presence of the Lord.

"The portion of Jacob is not like them: for he is the former of all things; and Israel is the rod of his inheritance: The LORD of hosts is his name". Jeremiah 10:16

Yet, when it comes to the Church, the Church is His bride, heavenly possession. The Church stands over the Israel and the Jews.

God fulfilled most of the covenants made to the children of Israel. The restoration of the kingdom unto them is yet to come.

Jesus will reign from the throne of David for one thousand years after restoration of the kingdom to them. Unto this end the 'great tribulation' lasts and unto this end the delay occurs in the coming of Jesus again.

Do not believe false prophets, false preachers, who predict the day of coming of Jesus. The Church will be 'caught up' when Jesus comes again.

For the Lord himself shall descend from heaven with a shout, with the voice of the archangel, and with the trump of God: and the dead in Christ shall rise first:

Then we which are alive and remain shall be caught up together with them in the clouds, to meet the Lord in the air: and so shall we ever be with the Lord. (1 Thessalonians 4:16-17)

CHAPTER 5

HAS GOD CAST AWAY

HIS PEOPLE

For I would not, brethren, that ye should be ignorant of this mystery, lest ye should be wise in your own conceits; that blindness in part is happened to Israel, until the fulness of the Gentiles be come in" (Romans 11:25)

Apostle Paul wonders if God cast away his people and immediately reaffirms that it was not so. He says he was also of the seed of Abraham, of the tribe of Benjamin. God did not cast away his people whom he foreknew.

Even when Elias was taking pride in himself that he was alone available to intercede on behalf of Israel God said to him that He had reserved seven thousand men unto him who could intercede on behalf of Israel.

If the salvation, therefore, is by 'grace', then it is not by 'works'. What then happened exactly that their attitude and belief has not changed yet? Yes, it is because God blinded their eyes for a season and gave them spiritual slumber that they should not see and that they may not have ears for hearing unto this day.

Have Israel stumbled that they should fall then? Apostle Paul himself answers these questions (Romans 11th Chapter) that God did not blind them or made them deaf because they were stumbling blocks nor was it because they have stumbled, but because of God's desire that everyone in the world, irrespective of Jews or Gentiles be saved and have eternal life.

This is the difference between the earthly Jerusalem and the New Jerusalem that comes down from heaven. John saw a new heaven and a new earth after the first heaven and the first earth passed away and there was no more sea.

In this New Jerusalem there was not seen any difference between Jews or Gentiles, but those who were there were all one in Christ. They had put on righteousness of Christ as their garments. They had received Jesus as their personal Savior and Lord by grace through faith in him.

More than any one taking pride of his belonging to any clan or sect the important fact that is to be borne in mind is that it is the grace of God that saves a man. No man needs precious metals such as gold and silver to earn a place in new Jerusalem, but all that a man needs is to have simple faith in Jesus, the Son of God, and make him Lord of his/her life.

God wipes away their tears. There shall be no more death, no more sorrow, and no more crying or pain. God shall give freely to all that thirst for such a life the fountain of life. He who overcomes the world and the temptations therein shall inherit the blessings from God and he shall be His son.

Apostle Paul explains elaborately the plan of God for the salvation of Gentiles in Romans 11th Chapter. Jews always insisted on recompensing God's favor with their own good works in order to earn salvation. They thought that their Messiah would come like a king. It is because of their misunderstanding that salvation is come unto the Gentiles.

"That at that time ye were without Christ, being aliens from the commonwealth of Israel, and strangers from the covenants of promise, having no hope, and without God in the world: But now in Christ Jesus ye who sometimes were far off are made nigh by the blood of Christ" (Ephesians 2:12-13)

CHAPTER 6

GREAT COMMISSION

"Go ye therefore, and teach all nations, baptizing them in the name of the Father, and of the Son, and of the Holy Ghost: Teaching them to observe all things whatsoever I have commanded you: and, lo, I am with you alway, even unto the end of the world. Amen" (Matthew 28:19-20)

The term "Great Commission" does not appear in the Bible, but just as we use few words/phrases in Christian common parlance to communicate certain meanings of the words like "Trinity", "Millennium", "Rapture", and "Bema Seat of Christ" the phrase "Great Commission" is used to convey the meaning that Jesus commanded his disciples to preach the Gospel.

There are four passages where we see the commandment of Jesus to preach the Gospel. Reading through Mark 16:15-18 some interpret that the commission given to the disciples is already fulfilled and that there is no commission in the present age to preach the Gospel.

Their argument is that the Word of God in itself is sufficient for someone to understand the Scriptures and no preaching is necessary. Their argument is that the disciples were asked to preach the Gospel and signs followed such preaching, and, since there are no signs followed in the present age the commission that was given in Matthew Chapter 28:18-20 is not valid. New Testament Church took birth as we read in Acts Chapter 2.

KINGDOM OF GOD

Jesus preached that the kingdom of God was at hand and the disciples who were sent two by two preached that men should repent.

"And they went out, and preached that men should repent. And they cast out many devils, and anointed with oil many that were sick, and healed them" (Mark 6:12-13)

The disciples of Lord Jesus Christ preached the Gospel of Jesus Christ only after they were empowered to speak with the power of Holy Spirit (Acts 1:4 & 8).

Later, Apostle Paul was chosen to preach the Gospel to Gentiles. Paul's ministry was basically intended for Gentiles, but the commission he received did not restrict him preaching to Jews in the beginning.

"But the Lord said unto him, Go thy way: for he is a chosen vessel unto me, to bear my name before the Gentiles, and kings, and the children of Israel" (Acts 9:15)

In fact, he preached to Jews and when they rejected him he went with message of salvation to Gentiles. This does not mean the Church came into existence after Acts 28:28.

After the ascension of Jesus and as the disciples were waiting they received the power to speak about Jesus. Earlier the disciples preached according to their knowledge thinking about the earthly kingdom of God. The disciples of Lord Jesus asked him as to when the kingdom would be restored to Israel but then Jesus said to them it was not for them to know the times and seasons which the Father had put in his own power.

John said: "John answered them, saying, I baptize with water: but there standeth one among you, whom ye know not". John 1:26

Mar 1:8 I indeed have baptized you with water: but he shall baptize you with the Holy Ghost.

DIFFERENT TYPES OF GOSPEL MESSAGES

Essentially the meaning of the "Gospel" is the "Good News". New Testament speaks of Gospel, which is the good news of the Lord Jesus Christ's bearing sin of mankind, His resurrection and ascension. This Gospel is preached in different forms and perspectives. There four different forms:

1. GOSPEL OF THE KINGDOM OF GOD

The Gospel of the 'Kingdom of God' that deals with the fulfillment of Davidic-covenant that the 'kingdom shall be established for ever before thee: thy throne shall be established for ever'. (2 Samuel 7:16). This Kingdom of

God includes the thousand year literal reign of Lord Jesus Christ from the throne of David in Jerusalem, as detailed in Zechariah 14:9 "And the LORD shall be king over all the earth: in that day shall there be one LORD, and his name one"

2. GOSPEL OF JESUS CHRIST

The 'Gospel of Christ' deals with the Salvation of mankind that Apostle Paul spoke of, as the 'Grace of God', that Jesus died for our sins, and that He was raised from the dead. Jesus died and was raised for our justification and we are justified because of our belief in Him. "For we stretch not ourselves beyond our measure, as though we reached not unto you: for we are come as far as to you also in preaching the gospel of Christ" (2 Corinthians 10:14)

3. THE GOSPEL CALLED "EVERLASTING GOSPEL"

The 'Gospel' that is called 'everlasting gospel', preached unto those, who did not believe in him, and who will pass through the 'great tribulation' until the last days before the last judgment. "And I said unto him, Sir, thou knowest. And he said to me, These are they which came out of great tribulation, and have washed their robes, and made them white in the blood of the Lamb". (Revelation 7:14)

4. THE GOSPEL CALLED "ANOTEHR GOSPEL"

The Gospel that is called 'another gospel', which is the perversion of the Gospel of Christ.

Christians are warned to be careful about this 'another gospel' by the agents of Satan, who transforms himself as the angel of light.

Apostle Paul writes about this gospel.

"I marvel that ye are so soon removed from him that called you into the grace of Christ unto another gospel: Which is not another; but there be some that trouble you, and would pervert the gospel of Christ". (Galatians 1:6-7).

False apostles calling themselves as apostles of Christ preach this gospel perverting the truth of the real gospel of Jesus that Apostle Paul calls as 'my gospel' in Romans 2:16, the gospel of Christ.

However, "my gospel" is not to be understood as Paul's personal Gospel, but it is the same Gospel which Peter and others preached; that is of Lord Jesus Christ's death, burial and resurrection.

Paul was contradicting those who were Judaizers, who insisted on circumcision for Gentiles to be saved.

This 'another gospel' dispels the efficacy of the blood of Jesus Christ and gives importance to law and works associated with it.

This gospel seeks to add works to faith in Christ. It shows that mere faith in Jesus is not enough to be saved but good works need to be done. While good works follow salvation, they are not conditional for receiving salvation.

Paul writes to the Church in Thessalonica that when they received the word of God, which they heard it from him, they received it not as the word of men, but as the truth from the word of God. He says that the truth of the Gospel will lead them to repent of their sins and help them to believe in Jesus Christ. (1 Thessalonians 2:13)

COMMISSION IN MARK 16:15-18

It would be good to ponder on Mark 16:15-18 before Matthew 28:18-20 is taken into consideration. The preceding verse of Mark 16:15 is about Lord Jesus Christ appearing to his disciples as they sat at meal and reproach them on their unbelief and hardness of heart.

The disciples obviously did not believe those things that had come to pass after the resurrection of Lord Jesus Christ.

After the resurrection Jesus appeared to Mary Magdalene, from whom Jesus had cast away seven devils (Luke 8:2 and Mark 16:9).

It was not to the Virgin Mary that Jesus appeared first but it was to this sinner woman who was redeemed by Jesus that he appeared first. There is a great comfort in knowing that Jesus has concern for sinners and for their redemption. The subsequent verses after Mark 16:18 say that Lord Jesus Christ was received up into heaven and sat on the right hand of Majesty on high. The disciples went forth and preached the Gospel everywhere.

Notice the word 'everywhere'. It does not confine to the regions of Jerusalem. As they preached the Gospel the signs followed them.

The signs were casting out devils, speaking in tongues, taking up serpents and that poison would not hurt them. Also, they shall lay hands on the sick who will recover, obviously meaning that they would be healed. (Mark 16:15-18)

The reason why some Christians say that there is no commission now is based on their belief that there are no such signs followed after preaching.

Here, we should remember that it was after resurrection when Lord Jesus Christ gave instructions that he said such signs will follow after preaching. But then, this commission in Mark 16:15-18 was intended for preaching to Gentiles. That message was only to Jews.

"An army chaplain once said to the Duke of Wellington, 'Do you think that it is of any use our taking the gospel to the hill tribes in India? Will they ever receive it?' The duke replied,

'What are your marching orders?' That was the only answer he gave. Stern disciplinarian as that great soldier was, he only wanted marching orders, and he obeyed; and he meant that every soldier of the cross must obey the marching orders of Christ, his great Commander." (Spurgeon)

Those who know about rules in the Armed forces will appreciate what Spurgeon was saying. Go forward without looking at the consequences.

Marching orders are to go ahead; no questioning. Some of Christians are out there now who say signs ceased so also the commission ceased. They say there is no 'Great Commission'.

COMMISSION BEFORE THE CRUCIFIXION OF JESUS

The commandment that Jesus gave to the disciples before he was crucified was in Matthew 10:5 "These twelve Jesus sent forth, and commanded them, saying, Go not into the way of the Gentiles, and into any city of the Samaritans enter ye not".

COMMISSION AFTER THE CRUCIFIXION OF JESUS

"But ye shall receive power, after that the Holy Ghost is come upon you: and ye shall be witnesses unto me both in Jerusalem, and in all Judaea, and in Samaria, and unto the uttermost part of the earth" (Acts 1:8).

Notice the phrase "after the Holy Ghost is come upon you". Acts 1:8 shows that the disciples were ordained to be the witnesses of Lord Jesus Christ first in Jerusalem, then in Judea and Samaria, and then in uttermost part of the earth.

The commission here says that the order of their being witnesses should be first among Jews in the regions of Jerusalem, and then in Judea and Samaria, which are the regions where Jews mixed up with Gentiles and then lastly to the uttermost parts of the earth, which means that they should be his disciples among the Gentiles in the uttermost part of the earth.

WERE THERE ONLY JEWS DURING PENTECOST?

It was feast time and there were men from every nation under heaven. The text in the following verses does not show that these all men were circumcised Proselytes.

Acts 2:5 And there were dwelling at Jerusalem Jews, devout men, out of every nation under heaven.

Acts 2:6 Now when this was noised abroad, the multitude came together, and were confounded, because that every man heard them speak in his own language.

Acts 2:7 And they were all amazed and marvelled, saying one to another, Behold, are not all these which speak Galilaeans?

Acts 2:8 And how hear we every man in our own tongue, wherein we were born?

Acts 2:9 Parthians, and Medes, and Elamites, and the dwellers in Mesopotamia, and in Judaea, and Cappadocia, in Pontus, and Asia,

Acts 2:10 Phrygia, and Pamphylia, in Egypt, and in the parts of Libya about Cyrene, and strangers of Rome, Jews and proselytes,

Acts 2:11 Cretes and Arabians, we do hear them speak in our tongues the wonderful works of God.

Acts 2:12 And they were all amazed, and were in doubt, saying one to another, What meaneth this?

Acts 2:13 Others mocking said, These men are full of new wine.

SEQUENCE OF PREACHING

The Word of God divides the sequence of preaching into three, that is, first in Jerusalem, second in Judea and Samaria and third in the uttermost part of the earth. We see the three stages in Acts from Chapters 1-7, second from Chapters 8 to 12 and third from Chapters 13 to 28.

The best possible sources identify that all the epistles of Paul were written during the time-period mentioned in Acts of Apostles.

In fact the Book of Acts does not record all the acts of all the disciples. This book mainly concentrates on some of the acts of Apostle Paul and some of the Acts of Peter. The Chronology of the epistles and the dates when they were written are disputable.

JESUS IS THE EXPRESS IMAGE OF THE FATHER

Hebrews 1:3 confirms that Lord Jesus Christ is the brightness of the Father and express image of His person, and upholds everything by the word of his power. He purged our sins and sat down on the right hand of the Majesty on high.

The argument of those who say that there is no Commission left in the present age is also based on these verses:

Acts 10:28, Acts 11:19-20, Gal.2:7-9, James 1:1

CORNELIEUS A GENTILE SAVED

It is worth considering each verse in its context. The whole Chapter 10 of Acts is about the Salvation provided for a Gentile named Cornelius. There are disputes in interpretations as to whether Cornelius was already a believer and Holy Spirit fell on him while Peter was yet speaking to him or he believed Jesus when Peter spoke to him and then the Holy Spirit fell on him.

HOLY SPIRIT FELL ON THEM

"While Peter yet spake these words, the Holy Ghost fell on all them which heard the word" (Acts 10:44)

Cornelius was just man who gave alms yet the angel of the Lord desired of him that he should be spoken to of the message of crucifixion and resurrection of Jesus signifying that his belief that being a just man and giving alms would not save him. After Cornelius heard this message Holy Spirit fell on not only on him but all them that heard the Gospel of Christ.

Marvelous are the ways of God who prepares His followers for His work. There was Cornelius a Gentile in God's sight.

Cornelius was a Centurion, who was just, giving alms and living a good life.

Bible says no good works will save a person; but only faith in Jesus will save a person. Here is a man who thought that his works are enough to be saved. But then, the angel of the Lord appeared to him in vision and told him that God has considered his alms and accepted his piety but then he should send forth men for calling Peter who was in Joppa and that he will tell Cornelius as to what he should do.

Simon Peter was staying at a tanner's house as recorded in Acts 9:43. A tanner is the one who does tanning and tanning is the process or art of converting skins into leather.

Basically the tanner is the one who deals with dead animals. According to Jews one that is dealing with dead animals is abominable. A woman in Jewish community is permitted to divorce her husband if he is involved with dead animals.

God was preparing his disciple Peter by allowing him to stay with a person who was dealing with dead animals. Peter was being prepared to approach Gentile Cornelius.

PETER WAS ASKED NOT TO CALL UNCLEAN

This was the time when Peter had a strange experience. He went up the housetop to pray and was very hungry.

He saw heaven opened and a certain vessel that was like a sheet came down with different kinds of four footed animals, fowls and creeping things on it. Peter heard a voice saying to him that he should rise, kill them and eat.

Peter was reluctant to eat them as he thought that they were unclean. This happened again, and the voice said to him that those which are considered as clean by God should not be considered as unclean by man. Peter refused to eat and this happened third time and the vessel taken up into heaven.

"But Peter said, Not so, Lord; for I have never eaten anything that is common or unclean. And the voice spake unto him again the second time, What God hath cleansed, that call not thou common". (Acts 10:14-15)

"And he said unto them, Ye know how that it is an unlawful thing for a man that is a Jew to keep company, or come unto one of another nation; but God hath shewed me that I should not call any man common or unclean". (Acts 10:28)

When Peter was thinking that it was a vision, there came men from Cornelius inquiring about Peter.

The Spirit of the Lord said to Peter that he should go to Cornelius and he went. Cornelius saw Peter and worshipped him by falling on his feet but then Peter lifted him immediately and said that he was a man like

Cornelius. That was to mean that only God is worthy of worship.

Peter said to him a man should not call any one as unclean if God has called him as clean. Peter testified about Jesus of Nazareth who died for all of us, and that God raised him on the third day.

As Peter was yet speaking Holy Spirit fell on them and they all marveled. Holy Spirit fell on the Gentiles as well. Please note very carefully the word 'Gentiles' is plural here.

That Is to say not only Cornelius but other Gentiles were also saved. This also should not be taken as an isolated case to call it as an exception.

It was indeed an opening door for Gentiles to receive the Gospel. "And they of the circumcision which believed were astonished, as many as came with Peter, because that on the Gentiles also was poured out the gift of the Holy Ghost". (Acts 10:45)

This is similar to what we see in Acts Chapters 1 and 2. It is wrong to presume that all the three thousand who were added unto them were Jews and it is also wrong to presume that Cornelius was grafted into Good Olive Tree about which Paul wrote in Romans chapters 9 through 11.

A Gentile does not need to be grafted into Good Olive Tree to become Jew first and then become a member of the body of Christ. Paul's comparison of Good Olive Tree and grafting of wild Olive branches is misunderstood by some. It is clear that Cornelius was an uncircumcised Gentile.

Cornelius conversion was, without any doubt, after the ascension of Jesus Christ into heaven. His conversion was by the hearing of the Word of God through Peter. He was saved by grace through faith in Jesus Christ, and not by any of His good works. Therefore, Cornelius's conversion was not proselytization to become Jew first and then a member of the body of Christ, but his conversion was a straight inclusion in the body of Lord Jesus Christ.

Apostle Paul's analogy of wild olive branches being grafted into natural olive tree is to mean that the Gentiles are made equal partners in the spiritual blessings along with Jews.

Some of the natural branches were cut off because of their unbelief and in their place the wild olive branches are grafted.

This is also not to mean that to accommodate Gentiles in the natural olive tree the branches of the natural branches were cut off, but because of their unbelief that the Jews, who are considered as natural olive branches, were cut off.

The wild olive branches are asked not to take pride in themselves because they were grafted into natural olive tree.

Paul warns that if natural branches were cut off because of their unbelief, God will not hesitate to cut off wild olive branches. This does not mean that salvation will be lost by any believer in Christ, but it only means that they will be cut off to make way for the natural branches.

An important thing here was that in the Old Testament period Jews were saved by their obedience God, but here in this New Testament period, Gentiles are given the privilege of salvation by the disobedience of Jews to the LORD. Gentiles are saved by grace through the faith in Lord Jesus Christ. Every Jew also has to come to God through Lord Jesus Christ for salvation.

Paul explains as follows:

"For I would not, brethren, that ye should be ignorant of this mystery, lest ye should be wise in your own conceits; that blindness in part is happened to Israel, until the fulness of the Gentiles be come in. And so all Israel shall be saved: as it is written, There shall come out of Sion the Deliverer, and shall turn away ungodliness from Jacob" (Romans 11:25-26 KJV)

Spiritually speaking "Not as though the word of God hath taken none effect. For they *are* not all Israel, which are of Israel" (Romans 9:6 KJV)

Salvation is by confessing by mouth that Jesus is Lord, and by believing in heart that God raised Him from the dead.

"That if thou shalt confess with thy mouth the Lord Jesus, and shalt believe in thine heart that God hath raised him from the dead, thou shalt be saved. For with the heart man believeth unto righteousness; and with the mouth confession is made unto salvation". (Romans 10:9-10 KJV)

Of course, this includes confession of sins to God through Lord Jesus Christ, who only is the mediator between God and man. There is no other mediator to bring reconciliation between God and man.

Peter was the first one to preach the gospel to Gentiles although Apostle Paul was called to be a minister for Gentiles. True to the words of Jesus who said, upon this rock I will build my Church, Peter was the first one to preach about Jesus of Nazareth in Acts Chapter 2 and Acts Chapter 10

"But ye shall receive power, after that the Holy Ghost is come upon you: and ye shall be witnesses unto me both in Jerusalem, and in all Judaea, and in Samaria, and unto the uttermost part of the earth" (Acts 1:8)

It is also wrong to presume that Jerusalem had only Jews during the period when Jesus was crucified.

Roman Government was in itself was not of Jews! In Acts Chapter 2 there is a mention that after the Pentecost was fully come in many people came to Jerusalem out of every nation under heaven.

HOUSE OF ISRAEL AND HOUSE OF JUDAH

After the captivity of the "House of Israel" and the "House of Judah" by Assyrians and Babylonians there is no evidence that "House of Israel" returned to Israel to contend that those who were in Samaria and other parts of Northern Israel were the seed of Jacob.

"And there were dwelling at Jerusalem Jews, devout men, out of every nation under heaven". (Acts 2:5)

Then they that gladly received his word were baptized: and the same day there were added unto them about three thousand souls. (Acts 2:41)

With regard to Acts Chapter 11:19-20 it is true that they began preaching to Jews only in the beginning but then according to verse 20 they spoke to Grecians and "preached the Lord Jesus".

That is to say from then onward they preached Lord Jesus to Gentiles as well. Likewise Peter was commissioned to preach to Jews while Apostle Paul was commissioned to preach to Gentiles as recorded in Acts 11:19-20 and in Galatians 2:7-9.

DID PETER WRITE TO GENTILES?

There is a greater evidence to show that Peter wrote to scattered Jews among Gentile Nations as we read in 1 Peter 1:1 but there is also an opinion that Peter wrote to Gentiles.

"Peter, an apostle of Jesus Christ, to the strangers scattered throughout Pontus, Galatia, Cappadocia, Asia, and Bithynia" (1 Peter 1:1).

The epistle was written somewhere around AD 60 before the Period of Acts ended in AD 63.

"Who his own self bare our sins in his own body on the tree that we, being dead to sins, should live unto righteousness: by whose stripes ye were healed". (1 Peter 2:24)

"Forasmuch as ye know that ye were not redeemed with corruptible things, as silver and gold, from your vain conversation received by tradition from your fathers; But with the precious blood of Christ, as of a lamb without blemish and without spot: Who verily was foreordained before the foundation of the world, but was manifest in these last times for you, Who by him do believe in God, that raised him up from the dead, and gave him glory; that your faith and hope might be in God". (1 Peter 1:18-21)

"And being brought on their way by the church, they passed through Phenice and Samaria, declaring the conversion of the Gentiles: and they caused great joy unto all the brethren. And when they were come to Jerusalem, they were received of the church, and [of] the apostles and elders, and they declared all things that God had done with them" Acts 15:3-4

"And when there had been much disputing, Peter rose up, and said unto them, Men [and] brethren, ye know how that a good while ago God made choice among us, that the Gentiles by my mouth should hear the word of the gospel, and believe". Acts 15:7

JAMES' ADDRESS SHOULD NOT BE MISCONSTRUED

James addressed in James 1:1 to the twelve tribes of Israel scattered abroad of their errors. He specifically wrote to the scattered twelve tribes of Israel, but then it was not to mean that Gospel of Jesus Christ was not preached to the Gentiles during that period. There is considerable exhortation to Gentiles in James 5:1-6

CHAPTER 7

POST-ACTS PERIOD

BELIEF

There is inconsistency in believing that Gospel of Jesus Christ was preached by only Apostle Paul to Gentiles based on Acts 28:27 and 28 and to presume that Paul's commission to take the message of salvation to Gentiles commenced after Acts 28:31.

"And upon the first day of the week, when the disciples came together to break bread, Paul preached unto them, ready to depart on the morrow; and continued his speech until midnight". (Acts 20:7)

"And after the uproar was ceased, Paul called unto him the disciples, and embraced them, and departed for to go into Macedonia. And when he had gone over those parts, and had given them much exhortation, he came into Greece, And there abode three months. And when the Jews laid wait for him, as he was about to sail into Syria, he purposed to return through Macedonia. (Acts 20:1-3)

Philip preached to Gentiles in Samaria. Ethiopian Eunuch was saved. (Ref: Acts Chapter 8). But then there are those who contend that all those in Samaria were of the seed of Jacob.

True there were Gentiles from the lineage of Jews in Samaria, but it is too much of an assumption to say that all those in Samaria were the seed of Jacob.

The text does not show that proselytes referred to in Acts Chapter 2 were circumcised ones; therefore, it cannot be conclusively said that they were equal to Jews; rather it is apt to say that they were a group of true proselytes and true Gentiles.

God has given enough material in the Scriptures for living a holy life. There were number of incidences shown in the Scriptures and those numbers are enough for us to believe without raising contradictions.

Not all the miracles done by Jesus are recorded in the Bible. Similarly not all the acts done by Peter and other disciples or by Apostle Paul were recorded.

GREAT COMMISSION AFTER ACTS 1:8

Lord Jesus Christ's own words in Matthew 28:18-20, Luke 24:44-49 and John 20:19-23 should be believed as the commission given to all of us to proclaim the Gospel of Jesus Christ to the best of one's capacity in the best possible way irrespective of any signs that may or may not follow the preaching.

It is misunderstanding that there is no commission for us to reach out to preach the Gospel of Jesus Christ. This Great Commission to preach the Gospel of Jesus Christ and that he is the savior of the world was preached by the disciples of Jesus Christ after waiting at Jerusalem and receiving the power of the Holy Spirit.

Apostle Paul was not there in Jerusalem when Holy Spirit came upon the disciples of Jesus Christ, but then, he was commissioned by Jesus Christ to go to the Gentiles signifying that all those who are called by God are required to be his witnesses and preach the Gospel of Jesus Christ and proclaim that he is the Savior of the world.

Jesus said "I am the way, the truth, and the life; no man cometh unto the Father, but by me". (John 14:6)

WHO CAN PREACH THE GOSPEL OF JESUS CHRIST?

"But ye are a chosen generation, a royal priesthood, an holy nation, a peculiar people; that ye should shew forth the praises of him who hath called you out of darkness into his marvellous light" (1 Peter 2:9)

"If any be blameless, the husband of one wife, having faithful children not accused of riot or unruly. For a bishop must be blameless, as the steward of God; not self-willed, not soon angry, not given to wine, no striker, not given to filthy lucre; But a lover of hospitality, a lover of good men, sober, just, holy, temperate; Holding fast the faithful word as he hath been taught, that he may be able by sound doctrine both to exhort and to convince the gainsayers". (Titus 1:6-9)

While woman may teach the word of God privately at home or in classes/meetings in women's fellowship Bible does not allow them to preach the Gospel of Jesus Christ in public or in Church.

But I suffer not a woman to teach, nor to usurp authority over the man, but to be in silence. (1Timothy 2:12)

Jesus said:

"And I say also unto thee, That thou art Peter, and upon this rock I will build my church; and the gates of hell shall not prevail against it". (Matthew 16:18)

"Now therefore ye are no more strangers and foreigners, but fellowcitizens with the saints, and of the household of God; And are built upon the foundation of the apostles and prophets, Jesus Christ himself being the chief corner stone" (Ephesians 2:19-20)

"For as the body is one, and hath many members, and all the members of that one body, being many, are one body: so also is Christ. For by one Spirit are we all baptized into one body, whether we be Jews or Gentiles, whether we be bond or free; and have been all made to drink into one Spirit. For the body is not one member, but many" (1 Corinthians 12:12-14)

Apostle Paul was the one who was sent out to preach the Gospel of Jesus Christ to the Gentiles. The salvation is by grace alone through faith in Jesus. Paul said circumcision is not required to be observed. Baptism is not part of salvation. Peter preached baptism as part of salvation but Paul did not preach baptism as part of salvation.

There were so much of legalism in Peter's preaching, but in Paul's preaching "Grace" is emphasized upon. This is not to say that they disagreed upon what they agreed upon to preach or preached different Gospels, but Peter basically was preaching in early days only to Jews while Paul preached to Gentiles.

"Then Peter said unto them, Repent, and be baptized every one of you in the name of Jesus Christ for the remission of sins, and ye shall receive the gift of the Holy Ghost". (Acts 2:38)

The only place where Paul's testimony that he baptized is found in Acts 18:8 and he acknowledged it in 1

Corinthians 1:14 "I thank God that I baptized none of you, but Crispus and Gaius"

And Crispus, the chief ruler of the synagogue, believed on the Lord with all his house; and many of the Corinthians hearing believed, and were baptized. (Acts 18:8)

THE COMMISSION TO PREACH THE GOSPEL OF JESUS CHRIST DID NOT END. IT WAS A NEW BEGINING IN ACTS CHAPTER 2 WHEN HOLY SPIRIT WAS POURED OUT AND THE CHURCH CAME INTO EXISTENCE. THE COMFORTER CAME INTO THIS WORLD AS WAS PROMISED AND HE WILL BE GONE AFTER THIS CHURCH AGE CEASES.

"And I will pray the Father, and he shall give you another Comforter, that he may abide with you forever" (John 14:16)

"All scripture is given by inspiration of God, and is profitable for doctrine, for reproof, for correction, for instruction in righteousness" (2 Timothy 3:16)

CHAPTER 7

GOD LOVES HIS

PEOPLE

"And I saw thrones, and they sat upon them, and judgment was given unto them: and I saw the souls of them that were beheaded for the witness of Jesus, and for the word of God, and which had not worshipped the beast, neither his image, neither had received his mark upon their foreheads, or in their hands; and they lived and reigned with Christ a thousand years" (Revelation 20:4)

God promised Abraham that in Isaac will be the blessed people who will be His people and He will be their God. Jesus came to save the children of Israel, yet they rejected him.

This paved the way for Gentiles to come to him for salvation and secure God's mercy. All those who had believed Jesus as their savior and laid faith in him were saved and likewise all those who believe in him shall be saved.

Two thieves were crucified one on either side of Lord Jesus. One of them mocked Jesus while the other sought mercy from Jesus.

He prayed that Jesus may remember him when He comes in his Kingdom.

Jesus said to the thief who prayed for mercy that he would be in Paradise the very same day when Jesus died on the cross.

Jesus was buried and he rose from the dead on the third day and later ascended into heaven. He is seated on the right hand of the Father in heaven. He will come soon. Salvation is available to anyone who calls upon Jesus for mercy.

Isaiah 40:11 "He shall feed his flock like a shepherd: he shall gather the lambs with his arm, and carry [them] in his bosom, [and] shall gently lead those that are with young".

Israel has become one nation in 1948 but they do not have the shepherd yet. They rejected Jesus as their Messiah and called for his blood to be upon them.

Has God forgotten Israel because they rejected him as their Messiah? No. God said

"Can a woman forget her sucking child, that she should not have compassion on the son of her womb? yea, they may forget, yet will I not forget thee". Isaiah 49:15.

The things are going to be worse for them that they will call for help from Jesus. He would not come until they realize that they have rejected him and they need him.

They will face terrible persecution under Antichrist in the last days. They would cry that the mountains may fall on them and kill them (Rev.6:16).

Israel will call upon God during the Great Tribulation period. God is not going to leave them but he will bring them on their knees to call upon his help. Then shall the Lord come to them and be their King of kings and Lord of lords. Jesus will reign for thousand years from the throne of David.

And I will give them an heart to know me, that I am the LORD: and they shall be my people, and I will be their God: for they shall return unto me with their whole heart. (Jeremiah 24:7)

God loved His people but they kept on rejecting him. The consequences, as Paul says, would be:

Tribulation and anguish, upon every soul of man that doeth evil, of the Jew first, and also of the Gentile; (Romans 2:9)

But, all those whose sins are washed in the blood of Jesus, irrespective of Jews or Gentiles will be caught up together to meet the Lord in the air even before the Great Tribulation starts.

"The dead shall rise first and we who are alive and remain shall be caught up together with them in the clouds to meet the Lord in the air: and so shall be ever be with the Lord" (1 Thessalonians 4:16-17)

Apostle Paul writes "For there is no difference between the Jew and the Greek: for the same Lord over all is rich unto all that call upon him". (Romans 10:12)

It is the Church that stands above Jew or Gentile finally and his saints as the bride of Jesus and as the Church that is going to be precious possession of Lord Jesus Christ.

CHAPTER 8

EVERYTHING HERE IS

DUNG

In the Old Testament the instructions given by God to Abraham to circumcise every male child on the eighth day was a covenant between God and Abraham. (A covenant is a mutual agreement).

God said every male child among the seed of Abraham after him, whether he is born in the house, or bought with money of any stranger, one that is not of Abraham's seed shall be circumcised and if anyone was not circumcised that soul shall be cut off from his people. It was equivalent to breaking the covenant.

This covenant was established by God between Him and Abraham that He will be God of Abraham and his posterity through Isaac. God promised Abraham that He will give him the land of Canaan as an everlasting possession. (Genesis 17:7-9)

For a New Testament believer circumcision profits nothing. Apostle Paul emphasized this fact in Romans 2:25

"For circumcision verily profits, if you keep the law: but if you be a breaker of the law, thy circumcision is made uncircumcision".

Referring to this circumcision, Apostle Paul writes in Philippians 3:4-8 that he was from the stock of Israel, of the tribe of Benjamin, a Pharisee, circumcised on the eighth day.

He says that if anyone has more trust in circumcision he would consider himself a better man than any other for having kept the law. He writes that, before he accepted Jesus as his Lord, he had great zeal to persecute the Church.

Paul's name was Saul before his conversion to follow Jesus. Perhaps, Paul would have gained wealth, name and fame if only he continued that which he was doing and in his status as a Pharisee, of the tribe of Benjamin, and with the pride of having been circumcised.

But, God's plan was not to let Paul into the world to earn some temporal benefits in this world, but His plan was to use Paul for His glory.

Paul says that he counted all the gain that he had in this world, or that which he would have had in this world by not accepting Jesus as his Savior was of no gain. He says it was all waste and loss.

The only thing that counted for him as gain was the excellence of the knowledge of Lord Jesus Christ, whom he called, as 'my Lord'. Paul calls everything of this world is just 'dung', a refuse.

"Yea doubtless, and I count all things but loss for the excellency of the knowledge of Christ Jesus my Lord: for whom I have suffered the loss of all things, and do count them but dung, that I may win Christ" (Philippians 3:8)

CHAPTER 9

SET AFFECTION ON

THINGS ABOVE

Many times when people think that their lives are best fortified the life quickly and easily ends and they leave behind their assets for someone else, not even their close ones, to enjoy.

King Solomon enjoyed every kind of blessing and was happy. He acknowledges that God loves a man who is good before Him.

He says all the days of a greedy man trying to earn more and more in his life are filled with sorrow, travail and grief with no rest in the night. He says God gives a man who is good in his sight wisdom, knowledge and joy, but to the sinner he gives travail, to gather up and to heap up more. He says it is vanity and vexation of spirit.

"For what hath man of all his labour, and of the vexation of his heart, wherein he hath laboured under the sun? For all his days *are* sorrows, and his travail grief; yea, his heart taketh not rest in the night. This is also vanity. *There is* nothing better for a man, *than* that he should eat and drink, and *that* he should make his soul enjoy good in his labour. This also I saw, that it *was* from the hand of God. For who can eat, or who else can hasten *hereunto*, more than I? For *God* giveth to a man that *is* good in his sight wisdom, and knowledge, and joy: but to the sinner he giveth travail, to gather and to heap up, that he may give to *him that is* good before God. This also *is* vanity and vexation of spirit' (Ecclesiastes 2:22-26 KJV)

Jesus questions how does it profit man who gains the whole world and loses his own soul? What could a man give in exchange for his soul? To be rich is not sin but fraudulent gain and cheating is sin. Trying to gain riches at the cost of working for God does no good. Matthew 16:26-28 say that Jesus will reward every man according to his works. Apostle Paul also says in 2 Corinthians 5:10 that we shall all stand before the judgment seat of Christ to receive rewards for working for Jesus.

It is indeed hard for a child of God to be in the world and be out of the temptations that this world brings into the lives of a believer.

The life in this world for a believer in Christ is not a bed of roses. Satan is always at work.

"And no marvel; for Satan himself is transformed into an angel of light". (2 Corinthians 11:14)

Unless a believer takes refuge in Christ and encounters Satan in the name of Jesus not even the best and strong believer would win over Satan. Believer has constant struggle against the desires of possession of wealth and not falling into lusts of this world.

THE ONE NEW MAN

The wise king Solomon drifted from his good path and married many wives and had concubines, More than his sin of being polygamist having married seven hundred wives, princesses and three hundred concubines he went after other gods namely Ashteroth, the Milcom (1 Kings 11:3 -5).

God promised that Solomon's throne will be established for ever and ever but He would chastise Solomon for his iniquity. (2 Samuel 7:13-14)

It so often bothers the mind of believer as how to clothe himself, how will he have food to eat and how his needs would be met with. Jesus asked to take a note of how the lilies of the field grow. He said they neither spin nor do they toil yet Solomon in all his glory was not arrayed like one of them.

Jesus asked to have faith that if God can clothe the grass of the field he shall clothe us too (Matthew 6:28-30)

It is, therefore, wise to do some works to gather for ourselves treasures in heaven where neither moth nor rust corrupts our wealth instead of storing up for ourselves treasures upon this earth where moth and rust corrupts and where thieves break through and steal. (Matthew 6:19-20)

Apostle Paul says if we are risen with Christ we should seek the things which are above where Christ sits on the right hand of God and not set our affection on the things on this earth.

"If ye then be risen with Christ, seek those things which are above, where Christ sitteth on the right hand of God. Set your affection on things above, not on things on the earth" (Colossians 3:1-2)

CHAPTER 10

WE ARE SAFE IN HIS

HANDS

Then touched he their eyes, saying, According to your faith be It unto you. (Matthew 9:29)

The blind receive their sight, and the lame walk, the lepers are cleansed, and the deaf hear, the dead are raised up, and the poor have the gospel preached to them. (Matthew 11:5)

Even though Jesus did miracles, yet Jews, who usually took delight in miracles, did not believe on Him as their Messiah, because they thought their Messiah would come like a king in a royal family. Contrary to their expectations Jesus was born as a poor man in the womb of Virgin Mary conceived of the Holy Ghost.

After Jesus grew up and started his ministry at the age of about thirty he chose few and called them to be his disciples. One such disciple was Matthew, who was a Publican; he collected customs and tax. Jews hated tax collectors because they were, in collaboration with authorities, harassing them. But then, this tax collector,

Matthew, found grace in the sight of the Lord, and he was called to be one of his disciples.

Matthew willingly accepted the calling from Jesus and instantly responded by following him. At one point of time, when Jesus was sitting with tax collectors and sinners, Pharisees, a learned sect of Jews, questioned him as to why he was sitting with them to eat.

When Jesus heard that question, he answered and said that those who are healthy do not need a physician, but they that are sick need physician. That was to tell them that the righteous do not need Savior, but sinners do need Savior. Basically, Jesus came for his own people, that is, the Jews; but then the salvation is extended to Gentiles also because Jews rejected Jesus as their "Messiah".

 The miracles that Jesus would do were prophesied in Isaiah 35:5-6 "Then the eyes of the blind shall be opened, and the ears of the deaf shall be unstopped. Then shall the lame man leap as an hart, and the tongue of the dumb sing: for in the wilderness shall waters break out, and streams in the desert". The prophecy was fulfilled when Jesus healed the sick.

God said to the children of Israel through Moses that if they "hearkened diligently to the LORD", the Lord would not bring upon them any of the diseases that He brought upon Egyptians (Exodus 15:26).

But they disobeyed God several times and their disobedience needed reconciliation. Adam rebelled against God by transgressing the commandment of

God. Bible records that we are all sinners by birth and there is no one righteous.

According to 1 John 1:8 "If we say that we have no sin, we deceive ourselves, and the truth is not in us". The Children of Israel transgressed the commandments of God several times.

In order to reconcile man with God, the Son of God, Jesus came into this world in the form of man to take upon our sins on him and die in our place that whosoever believes on him shall receive salvation and be saved from eternal damnation. God loved man so much that He gave his one and only Son, Jesus Christ that whoever believes in him shall be saved.

Friend, are you burdened with the thought that your sin is too great that it cannot be forgiven? Please be sure that every sin, except blasphemy of the Holy Spirit, is pardonable by God.

"Come unto me, all ye that labour and are heavy laden, and I will give you rest" (Matthew 11:28)

www.ingramcontent.com/pod-product-compliance
Lightning Source LLC
Chambersburg PA
CBHW021138020426
42331CB00005B/820